ASTROLOGY

SCORPIO

BY ABBY DOTY

Apex is distributed by North Star Editions:
sales@northstareditions.com | 888-417-0195

Produced for Apex by Red Line Editorial.

Photographs ©: Shutterstock Images, cover (illustration, constellation), cover (background), 1, 4–5, 6–7, 9, 12–13, 15, 16–17, 18–19, 20, 21, 22–23, 26–27, 29; Tami Kauakea Winston/Photo Resource Hawaii/Alamy, 8; Bettmann/Getty Images, 10–11; iStockphoto, 14; Kevin Sabitus/Getty Images Sport/Getty Images, 25

Library of Congress Control Number: 2025939155

ISBN
979-8-89250-789-9 (hardcover)
979-8-89250-818-6 (paperback)
979-8-89250-875-9 (ebook pdf)
979-8-89250-847-6 (hosted ebook)

Printed in the United States of America
Mankato, MN
012026

NOTE TO PARENTS AND EDUCATORS

Apex books are designed to build literacy skills in striving readers. Exciting, high-interest content attracts and holds readers' attention. The text is carefully leveled to allow students to achieve success quickly. Additional features, such as bolded glossary words for difficult terms, help build comprehension.

TABLE OF CONTENTS

CHAPTER 1

THE SCORPION

Scorpius is a **constellation**. Its name means “scorpion” in Latin. The stars curve in a hook shape. The end forms the scorpion’s tail.

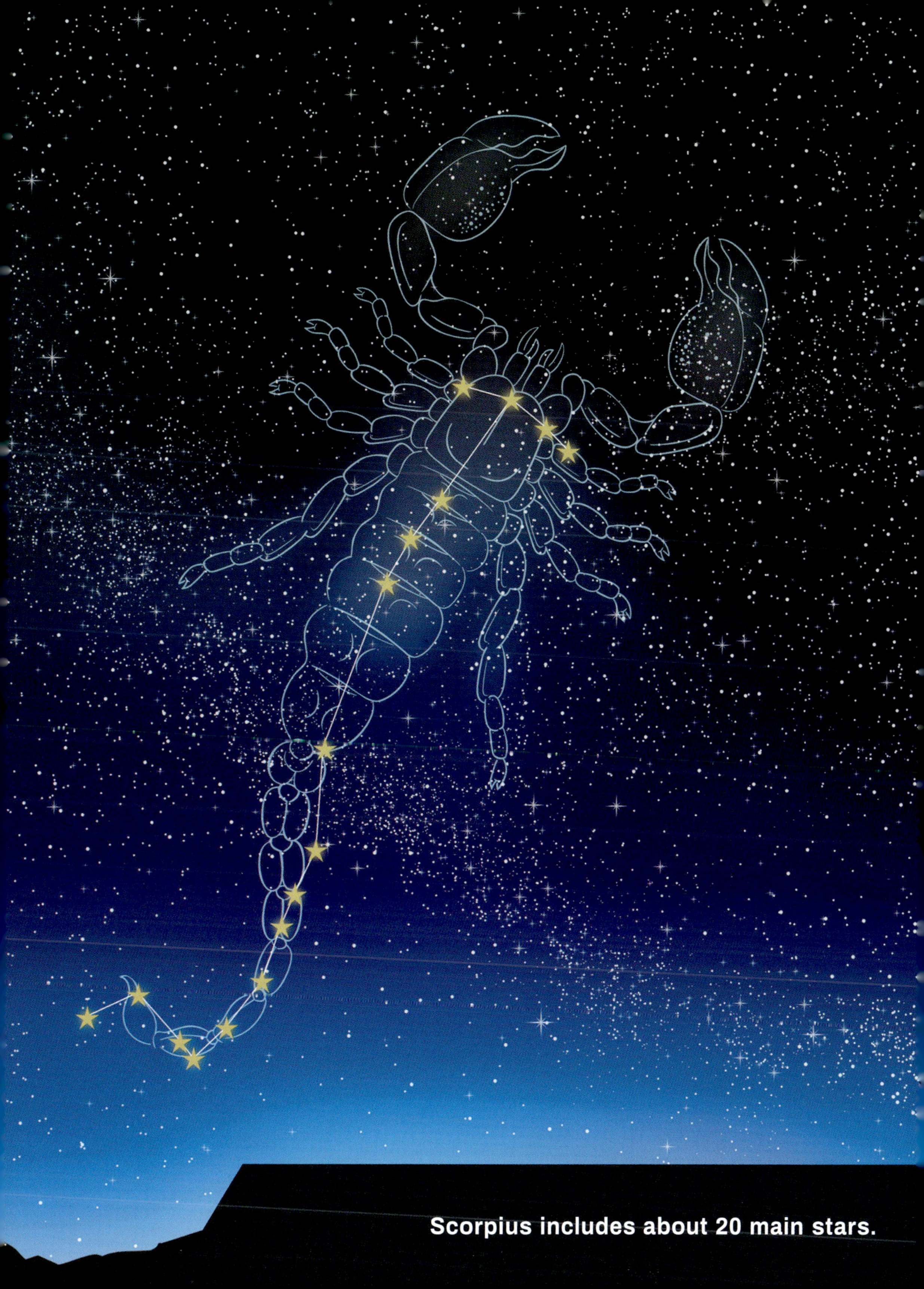

Scorpius includes about 20 main stars.

The ancient Greeks told stories about Scorpius. In one, Orion the hunter said he could kill every animal. A goddess sent a scorpion after him. It stung and killed him.

OPPOSITES

In the northern **hemisphere**, people can see the constellation Orion in the winter. In the summer, they can see Scorpius. It's like the constellations are chasing each other. When one appears, the other goes away.

The Greeks said the god Zeus placed Orion and Scorpius on opposite sides of the night sky.

In Hawai'i, fishhooks are often made from wood or bone.

Hawaiians said Scorpius was a fishhook. The hero Māui used the hook to pull up land from the sea. That land formed the Hawaiian Islands.

FAST FACT

In Indonesia, people described Scorpius as a swan or a leaning tree.

Some coconut trees grow at a sharp slant. In Indonesia, people compare Scorpius to this shape.

CHAPTER 2

SIGNS AND SEASONS

There are 12 **zodiac** signs. Each sign is based on a constellation. Scorpio is the eighth sign. It is based on Scorpius.

The signs of the zodiac are based on old ideas about objects in space.

Each sign has its own time of year. Scorpio's time begins around October 24. It ends around November 21. People born during this time have Scorpio as their **sun sign**.

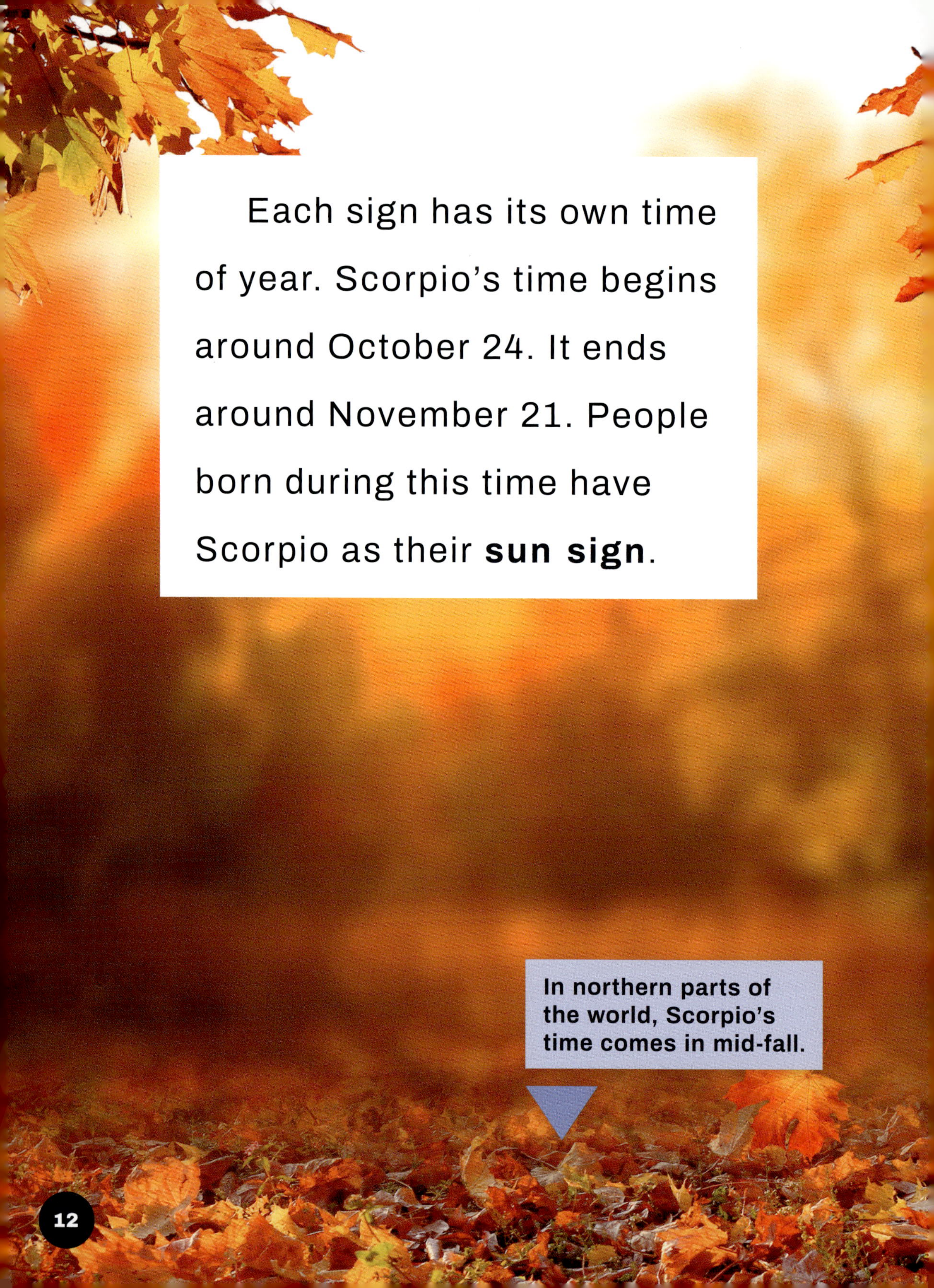

In northern parts of the world, Scorpio's time comes in mid-fall.

FAST FACT

Scorpio is a fixed sign. That means its time comes in the middle of a season.

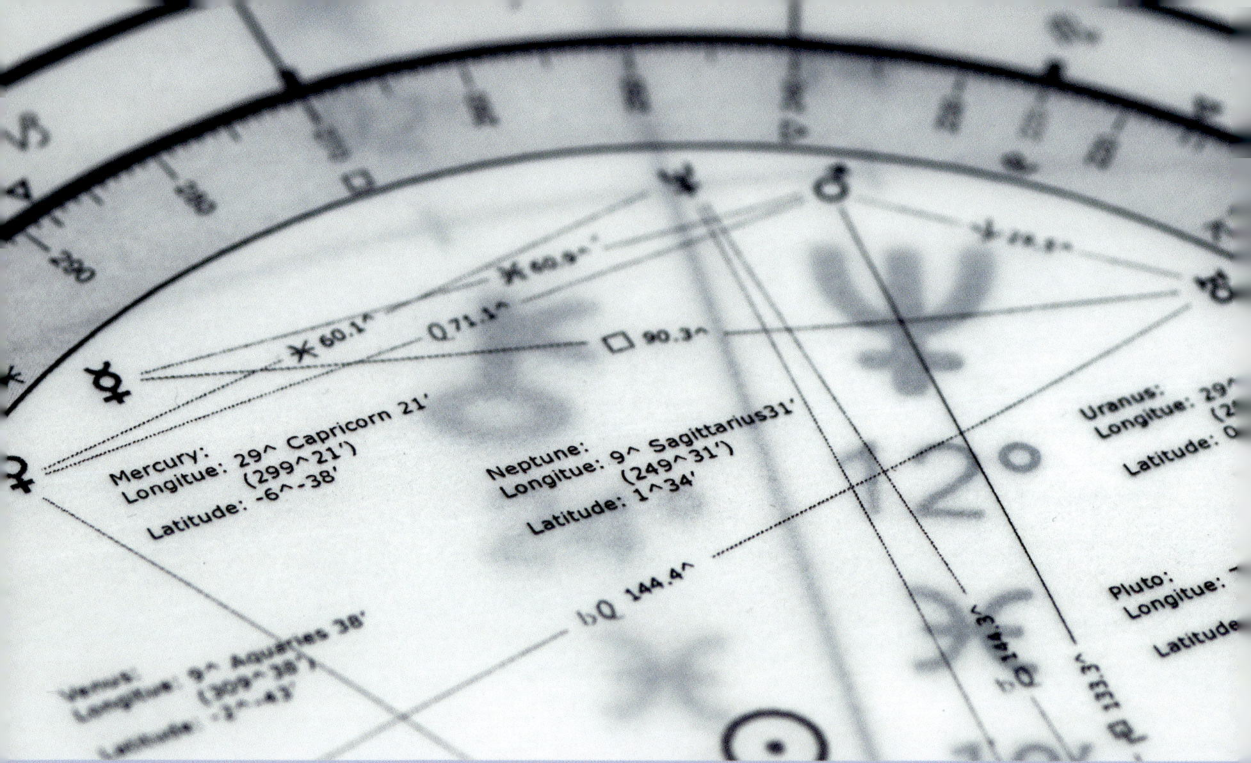

A birth chart shows where different planets were when someone was born.

Besides a sun sign, each person also has several other signs. Astrology claims that each sign reveals a different part of someone's **personality**.

THE BIG SIX

Each person has six main signs. These include sun, moon, Mars, Mercury, and Venus signs. The sixth is a rising sign. It's based on what time of day the person was born.

Mercury signs are said to shape how people think and talk.

Venus signs are said to show what people love.

CHAPTER 3

ABOUT SCORPIO

Each zodiac sign has a **glyph**. Scorpio's glyph looks like an M with a curved arrow. The arrow represents the scorpion's stinger.

The glyph for Virgo also looks like an M. But it ends in a loop.

Each sign also has an **element**. Scorpio's is water. Water signs are known for having deep emotions. And Scorpios tend to have strong feelings.

GUT FEELINGS

Water signs are said to have good intuition. That means they can figure out what others are thinking or feeling. Scorpios often use that information to make choices and plans.

Scorpios may hide their feelings. But like the ocean, they often have lots going on below the surface.

In astrology, the planet Mars is said to shape what people want and how they go for it.

At first, Scorpio had Mars as its ruling planet. This planet was said to shape how Scorpios act. But then scientists discovered Pluto. Now, Pluto rules Scorpio.

FAST FACT

In astrology, Pluto is linked to power and change.

Pluto is a dwarf planet. It's named after a Roman god who ruled the land of the dead.

CHAPTER 4

SCORPIO PERSONALITY

Scorpios are known for being private. They can take a while to open up to people. But once they do, they can be extremely **loyal**.

Just as a scorpion's tough shell protects its body, Scorpios may be guarded about their feelings.

Astrology also says that Scorpios work hard for what they want. They have clear goals. And they do not give up easily.

FAST FACT

Famous Scorpios include SZA, Ryan Gosling, and Amon-Ra St. Brown.

Training hard every day helped Amon-Ra St. Brown become one of the best receivers in the NFL.

Scorpios often enjoy jobs where they can learn, lead, and ask questions.

Sometimes, Scorpios can be controlling. They may want to tell others what to do. But they can learn to let go and trust others.

SCORPIO JOBS

Many Scorpios enjoy solving problems. They like finding out information. And they're not afraid of challenges. So, they may get jobs that involve science or medicine.

COMPREHENSION QUESTIONS

Write your answers on a separate piece of paper.

1. Write a few sentences explaining the main ideas of Chapter 2.

2. Do you find it easy to set and reach goals? Why or why not?

3. What was Scorpio's first ruling planet?

    A. Mars
    B. Venus
    C. Pluto

4. Who might a Scorpio be most likely to open up to?

    A. a friend they have known for years
    B. a new classmate from their school
    C. a person that they just met

5. What does **represents** mean in this book?

*Scorpio's glyph looks like an M with a curved arrow. The arrow **represents** the scorpion's stinger.*

A. looks like
B. breaks apart
C. hides

6. What does **solving** mean in this book?

*Many Scorpios enjoy **solving** problems. They like finding out information. And they're not afraid of challenges.*

A. causing
B. fixing
C. ignoring

Answer key on page 32.

GLOSSARY

constellation
A group of stars that form a shape.

element
One of four forces (air, earth, fire, or water) that each zodiac sign is matched with and said to be shaped by.

glyph
A shape that stands for a word or idea.

hemisphere
One half of planet Earth.

loyal
Loving and staying true to a person.

personality
The way a person usually acts.

sun sign
A person's main zodiac sign, which is decided by the date they were born.

zodiac
The set of 12 signs used in astrology, based on a part of the sky that the sun appears to move through each year.

TO LEARN MORE

BOOKS

Betts, Bruce. *Mars: The Red Planet*. Lerner Publications, 2025.

Goldstein, Margaret J. *Mysteries of Stars*. Lerner Publications, 2021.

Loh-Hagan, Virginia. *Star Signs*. Cherry Lake Publishing, 2021.

ONLINE RESOURCES

Visit **www.apexeditions.com** to find links and resources related to this title.

ABOUT THE AUTHOR

Abby Doty is a writer, editor, and booklover from Minnesota. Her sun sign is Aquarius.

INDEX

ANSWER KEY:
1. Answers will vary; 2. Answers will vary; 3. A; 4. A; 5. A; 6. B